CONSIDERATIONS CONCERNING THE PRESENT ENGAGEMENT

by

JOHN DURY

Published by *The Rota* at the University of Exeter
1979

© The Rota, 1979

ISBN : 0 904617 12 2

The Rota is an independent, academic society,
wholly supported by its subscribers.
Its sole purpose is publication of facsimiles,
of British tracts of the Stuart era.

This is the twenty-second pamphlet published by *The Rota*.
For more information please contact
Maurice Goldsmith or Ivan Roots
at the University of Exeter.

Printed in Great Britain by
The Printing Unit of the University of Exeter

PREFATORY NOTE

By trying and executing the king for high treason the Rump of the Long Parliament found themselves in the awkward position not of having to set up a new constitution — for they could carry on much as before — but of finding some means of securing the voluntary obedience of reluctant and conscientious citizens. The sword was clearly necessary but it could hardly be held at everyone's throat. The Rump sought to justify what had been done by rehearsing, in *A declaration of the Parliament of England, expressing the grounds of their late proceedings, and of setling the present government in the way of a free state* (22 March 1649), the claim that the actions were taken for the people against the tyrannical Charles Stuart, but it was also thought possible to advocate obedience without actually accepting the government as legitimate. This view was expressed in Francis Rous's *The lawfulness of obeying the present government* (25 April 1649). Rous announced himself 'one who loves all Presbyterian lovers of Truth and Peace, and is of their communion'. To those who could not swallow the recent *Declaration* and regard the government as lawful, Rous, following Calvin, advised on the authority of St Paul, *Romans* 13, submission to the possessors of *de facto* power. Rous's pamphlet touched off a controversy which was given further impetus when the Rump extended the oath of allegiance, originally designed for members of the Council of State, first, to almost anyone holding almost any sort of public office or position (11 October 1649), and then, (2 January 1649/50) to all male citizens of 18 years or above. The focus of the argument shifted to the question of whether Englishmen were not only obligated to obey the government but also whether they could swear the 'Engagement' to be 'true and faithful to the Commonwealth of England, as it is now Established, without a King or House of Lords'.

John Dury, (or Durie) the indefatigable campaigner for Protestant unity and peace, connected with Samuel Hartlib and his circle, had briefly served as tutor to Princess Mary in the Hague in 1642-43, but returning to England, had been one of those who drew up the Westminster Confession. He now emerged among the government's strongest supporters in the engagement controversy. *Considerations concerning the present engagement, whether it may be lawfully entered into; yea or no?* (dated by Thomason 4 December, though both the imprimatur and Dury's signature are dated 27 November) was one of Dury's (at least nine) contributions. (He had already published a precursor, *A case of conscience resolved: concerning ministers medling with state matters in their sermons*, dated 29 March, though the imprimatur of 15 March shows that it was written before the *Declaration* was published. The second edition of 8 November is greatly enlarged.) Dury's *Considerations concerning the present engagement* argues that either the engagement is consistent with the previous oath of allegiance and the Covenant, or those obligations have been extinguished. In any case, God has ordained (see *Romans* 13) that subjects, private men, should not dispute but obey those in supreme and plenary possession of power, whether it had been acquired by contract or by conquest (p. 15). Moreover God's providence has placed the current regime in authority. Finally, fidelity (at least in lawful things) is owed to those from whom we actually receive protection (p. 18), an argument possibly derived from another notable controversialist, Anthony Ascham. Among others involved in the dispute were Marchamont Nedham, William Prynne, Edward Gee, Robert Sanderson, John Lilburne and Gerrard Winstanley. The controversy prompted the publication of Thomas Hobbes's *De corpore politico* (which with *Humane nature* formed *The elements of law, natural and politic* written in 1640) and evoked the translation (not in fact by Hobbes himself) and printing of his *Philosophicall rudiments concerning government and society* (*De cive*). The dispute provided the ideological context in which *Leviathan* was read.

Considerations concerning the present engagement is one of the most frequently cited engagement tracts. It went through four editions; the first, here reprinted, runs to 24 pp. to which is added in some copies an errata list. The second edition is reset in 22 pp. The third edition (in print by 21 February 1649/50) and the fourth (by 4 April 1650) both include a letter replying to someone raising the scruple of obligations imposed by former oaths contradicting the engagement. (Both the errata sheet and the letter are included in *The Rota* facsimile.) The letter is the only substantial amendment in later editions, though there are some corrections and changes in typographical style along with the usual incidence of new errors.

The bibliography of the engagement controversy has been admirably compiled by John M. Wallace, 'The engagement controversy 1649-1652: an annotated list of pamphlets', *Bulletin of the New York Public Library* LXVIII (1964), 384-405; and see his *Destiny his choice: the loyalism of Andrew Marvell* (Cambridge, 1968), pp 43-68. See also Quentin Skinner, 'History and ideology in the English revolution', *Historical Journal* VIII (1965), 151-78; 'The ideological context of Hobbes's political thought', *ibid.* IX (1966), 286-317; and 'Conquest and consent: Thomas Hobbes and the engagement controversy' in G. E. Aylmer (ed.), *The interregnum: the quest for settlement, 1646-1660* (London, 1972); and P. Zagorin, *A history of political thought in the English revolution* (London, 1954), pp. 62-77.

Considerations concerning the present engagement (Wing D2842, Wallace 18), is reprinted with the permission of the Curators of the Bodleian Library from the following: G. Pamph. 2337(29) for pp. 1-24; 4° E. Jur. (8) for the errata page; Pamph. C. 90(30), third edition, for the letter, additional pp. 23-26.

CONSIDERATIONS
Concerning the present
ENGAGEMENT,
WHETHER
It may lawfully be entered
into; YEA or NO?

Written at the desire of a friend, by J. D.

JOHN 3. 21.
He that doth the Truth comes to the light.

November 27. 1 6 4 9.
Imprimatur, JOSEPH CARYL.

LONDON,
Printed by *John Clowes* for *Richard Wodenoth,* at the
Starre under St. Peters Church in
Cornhill, 1 6 4 9.

CONSIDERATIONS
CONCERNING
The present Engagement.

SIR,

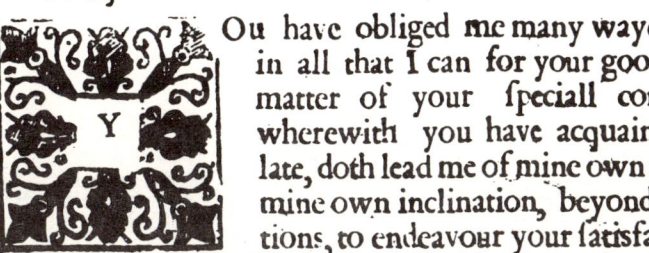You have obliged me many wayes to serve in all that I can for your good; but the matter of your speciall concernment, wherewith you have acquainted me of late, doth lead me of mine own accord, by mine own inclination, beyond all obligations, to endeavour your satisfaction. Seeing then your conscience is scrupled about the engagement which by the Parliament is offered to be taken, and you say you cannot subscribe thereunto, till three main doubts concerning the same be cleared; I shall take them into serious consideration, to shew you what I think of the weight thereof, which indeed is of exceeding great moment. For you say, 1. That the Oath of Allegiance, and the Nationall Covenant are still binding, and contradictory to this present engagement.

2. That the present Power by which the engagement is tendered, is very doubtfull, as a power unlawfully usurped; to which usurpation you think you will be accessary if you take the Engagement.

3. That the consequence of the Engagement, seems to tend to an opposition against the lawfull Heir of the Crowne, and the

the right constitution of the Parliaments, whereunto you are pre-engaged, and from which you cannot recede.

To satisfie your desire, I shall lay before you, as briefly as may be, my sence thereof, that you who have been alwaies welaffected to the common cause of Liberty, against the designs of Tyrany may be helped somewhat, to discerne how lawfull or unlawfull, how expedient or unexpedient, it will be for you, to take, or not to take this Engagement for the publick good, and the discharge of your duty towards the same.

First then, concerning the Oath of Allegiance, and the Nationall Covenant, represent unto your self the true meaning thereof, and so order your thoughts to do that which is answerable thereunto.

The Oath of Allegiance, as you know, did bind all men as Subjects in Law, to be true and faithfull to the Kings Person, to his Heirs and Successors, as they were invested with the Authority which the Law did give them: nor was it ever meant by the Parliament which Enacted the Oath of Allegiance, that any should be absolutely bound to the King & his Heirs, as they were men, to be true and faithful to their personal wils, but only to them & their wils as they had a Legall standing: that is, to the Authority conferred upon them by the consent of the People, which was testified in & under a Law; whereunto the King and his Heirs were bound for the Kingdoms good by Oath: So that the obligations of King and subjects are mutuall, and must needs stand and fall together, according as the condition by which they are begotten is kept or broken; which is nothing else, but the Law according to which he and his Subjects agree, that he shall be their King, and they shall be his Subjects. For as you were sworn to the King, so he was sworne to you: as you were bound to be faithfull to him, so he was bound to be faithfull to his trust: nor is he your Liege further then he is faithfull thereunto. If then he be found unfaithfull to his trust, you are *ipso facto*, absolved from your Allegiance unto him;

and

the present Engagement.

and if according to Law he receives not his Authority, you are not in Law his Subject at all. Now the just and naturall foundation of all Lawes, is the reason of the Body, of every Nation in their Parl. which hath the sole Right to propose & chuse the Lawes, by which they will be Ruled. Whence it hath been (as I suppose) a perpetual custome in this Nation, for the Commons at all times to aske and propose the making of Laws; and for the Lords and King, to give their consent thereunto: the Lords as the Judges in cases of transgression, and the King as the executer, and publick Trustee, for the administration of the common good and wealth thereby; for in a Kingdom there is a Common-wealth, as the intrinsicall substance of the Being thereof; for which all things are to be done by King and Lords, as the publick servants thereof; and Ministers not Masters of State therein. If the King then should set himselfe wilfully to be above this Reason of the Nation, which is the onely Originall of the Law, and refuse obstinatly the Lawes, which they shall chuse to be setled: he puts himself *ipso facto*, out of the capacity of being a King any more unto them, and if this can be made out, to have been the way wherein the late King set himself, and that it was the designe of the House of Lords, to uphold and enable him to follow that way: it is evident, that so far as he did by that means actually un-King himselfe as to this Nation: so far also, they that assisted him in that designe, did un-Lord themselves in the State thereof, and if this was the guilt of the house of Lords by other practises and proceedings more than by an indifferency and complyance with the *Hamiltonian* invasion, to help the King to such a Power, I know not what to answer for them.

But as to the meaning of the oath of Allegiance, as by the perpetuall consent of all ages, it never was otherwise understood; and by the third Article of the Nationall Covenant, (which is another branch of this doubt) may be made manifest. It is then undeniable, that the third Article of that Nationall Covenant,

was

was never meant by those that made it, or that took it, to be oppofite to the fence of the Oath of Allegiance; but altogether agreeable thereunto. What then the meaning of that Article is, muft needs alfo be the true fence of the Oath of Allegiance. That Article then doth oblige you, to preferve the Right and Priviledges of the Parliament, and the Liberties of the Kingdom in your Calling, abfolutely and without any limitation; but as for the Kings Perfon and Authority, it doth oblige you onely thereunto, conditionally and with a limitation; *Namely in the prefervation and defence of the true Religion and Liberties of this Kingdom*: If then the King did not give to the Reprefentatives of the Nation that affurance which was fatisfactory and neceffary, that their Religion and Liberties fhould be preferved, none but his Subjects were bound either by their Allegiance or Covenant, to defend his Perfon and the Authority, which was conferred upon him. The Oath of Allegiance therefore was bottomed upon the Laws, which the Reprefentatives of the Nation in Parl. had chofen to be obferved concerning their Religion, and the Liberties of the Kingdom; which he refractorily either cafting off, or feeming to yield unto, in fuch a way that no truft could be given him, that he would keep what he yeilded unto; the Parliament did actually lay him afide, and voted, that no more Addreffes fhould be made unto him: from which time forward he was no more an object of your Oath of Allegiance, but to be lookt upon as a privat man: and your Oath by which you were engaged, to be true and faithfull to the Law, by which the Religion and Liberty of the Kingdom was to be preferved, did ftill remaine in force: which if it may be the true fubftantiall fence of the prefent Engagement, which you think is contradictory to this Oath and to the Nationall Covenant, then you are to look well to it, that you be not miftaken. For to an indifferent eye, it may be thought fo far from being oppofite to the true fence of either, that it may be rather a confirmation of the ground; for which

both

the present Engagement.

both the Oath of Allegiance, and the third Article of the Nationall Covenant was then binding; For the ground of all these Obligations, is nothing else, but the welfare of the Commonwealth, which was intrinsicall, to that which was called the Kingdom, to which you are bound by the Law of Nature and Nations, to be true and faithfull for it self, and to the King, to the particular Laws whereof the King is a servant to keep them and see them kept; and to the Liberties, which by Law were limited (lest they should be exorbitant) and preserved, (lest they should be incroached upon) you were bound for that Common-wealths sake, which in the bosome of the Kingdome was then, and is now without it exstant, and in being by it self. So then it may seeme that you are so far from being put by this Engagement upon any Declaration contradictory to your former Oaths, that you are rather obliged thereby to stand firme to the same, by the fundamentall Reason thereof, as it is wrapt up in the common cause of Religion and of the Liberty of the Nation: which notwithstanding any alterations which are fallen out, or may fall out hereafter are to be constantly and unalterably preserved: for this or that outward forme of Government, is wholly accidentall, and no waies essentiall to any Nation of the world: and therefore is alterable, in respect of formes, as is most expedient for their exigent necessities; but to be governed by Lawes, and to have the use of the true Religion, and of the Nationall Freedom, is absolutly necessary, and essentiall to the being of a Commonwealth.

It may bee conceived then that the intent of the Engagement is to this effect; that seeing there is still a Nationall tye and Association remaining amongst the people of this land; whereof the Common good ought to be procured truly, and faithfully by all that belong thereunto; therefore you are required to declare, that the want of that accidentall forme of Government, which stood in the having of a King and House of Lords, shall not take you off from being willing to procure

the

the same : which I thinke you are bound in conscience, as to intend, so to declare and really to endeavour.

But you will press this further and say, that in the third Article of the Covenant you are sworne to preserve the Rights & Priviledges of the Parl. now (say you) amongst the Rights & Priviledges of the Parl. this is one; that therin should be a house of Lords distinct from the Commons, and this another, that all the Members of the Commons should sit and Vote freely; for when you swore, you meant a Parliament so constituted, and none other: but now (say you) I am put upon a Declaration contrary to the intent of that part of my Oath: because I am obliged to be true and faithfull to the Common-wealth, as it is without such a House, and such Members of the Commons.

To examine this Scruple I shall grant materially all that you say; First concerning your sense of the Rights and Priviledge of Parliament. Secondly the present Parliament that it is not such as the former was without any alteration. Thirdly concerning the intention, which you say you had in that Part of your Oath : that it cannot now be prosecuted to that effect, whereunto you say you tooke it; for if you tooke it, to preserve those Rights of Parliament which you have mentioned; it must be granted that such an intention cannot now be prosecuted by you in your privat calling: But yet for all this which I have granted, I must say that the taking of the present Engagement, will not make you more guilty of the breach of this part of your Covenant than you are already : for if you did when time and place was, according to your calling, what in you lay, to prevent the breach of those priviledges; you did observe your Covenant, & cannot be accused of the infringement thereof; for when a fatall necessity of State; in the course of Divine Justice, with a power irresistable, not only to men of privat, but to all that were in publick vocations, did bring about that Change upon the Parliament, no particular mens engagements were considerable. Therefore of that charge, whether you attempted, or attempted not to hinder it, you cannot be counted

guilt

the present Engagement.

guilty; what ever the intent of your promise was in the Covenant, because it was neither morally possible nor lawful to you in the way of your calling, to hinder the cause or effect of that change; and therefore to you it cannot be imputed as a breach of Covenant. But you will here say, true indeed I am not guilty; but others in my opinion are: But if I promise now to be true and faithfull to the Common-wealth, as upon this breach of priviledge they have setled it, then I confirme what they have done, and so make my self accessary to their guilt and breach of Covenant. Here I perceive is that which doth pinch you in the busines: you thinke, they that made the change broke the Covenant, & if you engage under this change, as is desired, you thinke you breake your Covenant also. To this I shall say; First, that they who made the change will plead for themselves, that they are not guilty of any breach of Covenant notwithstanding that change; but this I shall leave to them to justifie, as not being needfull for the resolving of your doubt at this time; therefore in the second place as to your self, I see not how it will appear, that the consequence which you draw from the act of the Engagement to the breach of Covenant, doth at all follow, although those that made the change should be guilty, as you think they are. And then also this I am confident of, to be able to let you see further, that although you may think that the effect of this Engagement is materially contrary to some intention which you had in the third Article of the Covenant; yet that by the act of the Engagement, you are so far from breaking your Covenant, that except you take it, and observe it faithfully, you will not onely materially, but formally break that very Article of the Covenant, for which you scruple the taking of the Engagement.

As for the consequence you make from taking the Engagement to a breach of the Covenant, it doth not at al follow to my understanding; for the direct & plain matter of the Engagement binds you onely to procure the good of the Commonwealth, as now it stands: and because at all times & in all constitutions

stitutions thereof, you are bound to do this; no lesse by the Covenant it self than by this Engagement; therefore your taking of this, to this effect, can be no breach of that. For the Negative words, *without a King and House of Lords*, (whereat you stumble) in the Engagement, may be properly and most obviously taken, as an explication of the words *Now established*, immediatly going before; and not an absolute abnegation of the things lookt upon truly as in themselves: so that the obvious meaning of the words, is to me as if they had been utterly thus assertorily. This Common-wealth at present doth stand without a King and house of Lords, and although it doth stand thus; yet I promise to be true and faithfull thereunto. Now it doth not at all follow, if I promise, to do my duty to the Commonwealth, although it is at this time thus setled; therefore I am accessary to all that hath been done to have it thus setled; Nor doth it follow, if I seek the good of the Common-wealth, although it wants a House of Lords; therefore I am accessary to the abolition thereof, or approve of the putting out of the Lords wholly from all share of Government in the Commonwealth. These things are altogether incoherent: for what ground is there for me to abstaine from doing my duty to the publick; because others have done (I think) more then theirs? Or because they do it not so as I can allow of it? Can their faultines one way, excuse my neglect of duty another way? To think so is very absurd, and therefore the consequence which you make, doth not at all follow.

But let us now go a step further, and suppose that in your apprehension of matters, this Engagement doth materially settle something in the Common-wealth, which is contrary to the intention which you had in taking the Covenant; yet I say, that by giving your assent thereunto, as matters now stand, you break not at all your Covenant, because your Obligation to those matters by vertue of the Covenant, was extinguished, before you were called upon to take this Engagement: now that which is extinct and made void, cannot be said to oblige a-
ny

ny more: and all promises are *ipso facto* made void and extinct, in respect of their tye upon the Conscience; when the thing promised, is become in it self impossible to be done, or in reference to our calling unlawfull to be prosecuted. It is impossible in nature to preserve the Kings life which is cut off, and the House of Lords which is already put down; And it is not lawfull for any in a private Calling to attempt the restoring of that which by publick power hath been abolished. Nor did the Covenant ever intend, to engage any to such an attempt: nor could any be lawfully obliged to intend such an undertaking: nor is there any word of restoring, but onely of preserving, in the Article of the Covenant. But if in your meaning, the promise of preserving should extend it self also to a restoring endeavour; yet still the limitation of this endeavour must be in and according to your Calling, not out of it, or beyond it: Now your Calling I suppose, at present, is only to acquiesce at the abolition of that which is made void, and not to declare any abrogation (as some would extend it) of the Right which the Lords have to sit in Parliament. They may have a Title to this Right, and yet be obliged, even for the preserving of that Right, which without an inevitable ruin to the publick wellfare cannot be obtained. Suppose that in order to the publick good, you were obliged by Oath to prosecute some busines, and that in following it, you should evidently perceive, that by the change of circumstances the prosecution of your businefs, intended for the good would prove the ruin of the publick; I say, that notwithstanding your Oath, by which you are engaged to follow such a busines, you are neverthelesse obliged to desist from it; because your Oath binds no further then it is evident that the publick good is advanced thereby; and if the change of circumstances alter the whole case of your businesse (as often in State-affairs it falleth out) I say your Oath is made *ipso facto* void; And thus the clause of the Covenant which relates unto the King & the House of Lords, as sworn in order to common welfare; if any should now prosecute by force, it is evident that he would by a new war hazard the ruining of al; which by all humane means possible in nature lawfull & not contradictory to the wil of God, we are al bound to the utmost to prevent; for to preserve the publick in peace & safety, is the main end of all the promises of the Covenant, whereunto all particular matters are subordinate; and if I should not suspend my particular pretentions to Right in order to publick safety, I transgresse the Covenant, which above all doth bind me unto this, which also is nothing else but the expresse sence of the Engagement which is now offered: so that the intent thereof, is no way contradictory, but altogether coordinate and consistent both with the Oath of Allegiance and the Nationall Covenant, so far as they are obligatory.

And to go yet a step beyond this consideration, I shall adde this, that if the third Article of the National Covenant concerning the Priviledges of Parl. be yet in force in any degree, as you suppose it is, then it binds you to preserve the priviledges of Parliament that now are, as well as those that then were. For if there hath not been a totall dissolution of all Government amongst us, but a Parl. notwithstanding all changes still kept up, and therein a right to rule and to order matters for the publick good preserved: then the Oath of preserving these Parl. Rights is still binding, so far as the Parl. is in being: nor can it be agreeable to the intent of that article, or to the rule of conscience, and of sound reason, that because it is supposed some have made a breach upon some of the Rights of Parliament; that therefore it should be free for any to break & dissolve all the rest. For if you count them guilty, who made void the Authority that then was in any degree, how can you be guiltlesse your self, if you intend to make void all that which remaines? Therefore so far as there is yet any ground of order & settlement in the Common-wealth by the Authority of Parliament, and by the Counsell of State and Courts of Justice depending thereon; you are by that very Covenant in Conscience still

bound

bound to preserve it: & to this very thing also the Engagement which is now offered doth clearly bind you; & (as I conceive) to nothing else directly; for the obvious sense of the express words can be none other but this: That so far as the Association of this people is setled, in a course of Government, and in the administration of Justice, you shall not overthrow but preserve the same, although the administration of this Government and justice is not now carried on by a King and House of Lords; but onely by the Parl. that now is, which certainly is your duty at this time; And if this is cleerly your duty for the publick good then you cannot understand the words of the Covenant to be binding in any other sense but in this; for the words must be taken in the sense which they can directly bear, and which do impart the main end for which the Covenant was taken; for the maine end of this very Article whereof you make a scruple, was evidently to preserve the Parliament and Common-wealth for it self, and (if need so required) also without the King.

Now this is that which the Engagement doth directly also require, for which cause I say, that by vertue of this very promise, you are bound to take the present Engagement; and if you take it not, that you make your self a transgressor of that very Article which you pretend to keepe; for if you refuse to be true and faithfull to the Common-wealth as it is now Established, you do what in you lyeth to make the remaining Rights of Parliament, and the beginnings of our settlement void; which though at first it was not intended to be without a King; yet it was clearly presupposed in the Article it selfe, as possible to be without him; and consequently, that although he should not be, yet that the Common-Wealth by the Rights of Parliament, and the Liberties of the Nation should be preserved; which is all that now is sought for by the Engagement.

I hope then that you shall find no cause to scruple any further at this; but that such as under the pretence of such scruples take a course to overthrow this Parliament, will be made conscionably awake to see their error; and that they Diametrically by such a purpose crosse the main intention of their Covenant, and become guilty of dissolving the whole tye of this Common-wealth. And this shall suffice concerning your first scruple at this time.

As concerning the present power by which the Engagement is tendered, your Doubt is, what you ought to think of it: whether you should count it a lawfull, or an unlawfull and usurped Power? and if such, whether you will not be accessary to their usurpation, by taking the Engagement?

To these Questions I shall answer distinctly, and let you see the Rules by which I order my conversation, in these cases, that if you have nothing to except against them, you may take them up, and walk in the righteousnes thereof.

For mine own part then, I have taken this to be a Rule, whereby all privat men (such as I am) as Christians ought to walk unblameably under the superiour powers of this world. Namely, *That it doth not belong to us, to judge definitively of the rights which the Supreame powers over us in the world, pretend to have unto their places.* And the Reason is this, because I finde it no part of the profession of Christianity to meddle with this matter, nor can I see that God doth allow privat men to take so much upon them over their Superiors, nor ought Superiors to suffer it in their Subjects, nor will sound reason, or a good Conscience allow it in any.

It is no part of our Christian profession, to become Judges of the great ones of this world, in respect of their rights and pretentions to power. For we are to behave our selves as spirituall men in this world, by the Rule of our profession, and as strangers and pilgrims therein. taking it as our passage to a Kingdome that cannot be shaken; and using it as the subject wherein our Faith & Patience, our mortification to things present and our hope for things to come are to be exercised. A stranger, passenger

senger & pilgrim, takes things as he finds them on his way, makes the best of them that he can, and meddles only with his own matters, how to advance prosperously, and easily towards his journeys end; that is, how to behave himself without blame and offence towards God and men, in all things, with a good Conscience: holding forth the Word of life, which is the Rule by which he doth walke in the feare of God towards others This is all that a Christian as a Christian, that is, by vertue of his Profession, is to meddle withall about the affairs of this world, which in so doing he doth judge in the spirit of righteousnes; but if he doth make himself a judge in another kind of particular rights & pretentions of the great ones in this world, he takes upon him that which doth not belong unto him in his Profession of Christianity, for he doth more then Christ would do on earth; for Christ our Master in this profession, would not become a Iudge of the least matters between man & man in the world; and how shall we that ought to be his followers and Disciples, take upon us, to judge of the greatest of all? How shall we Answer this to him? Is not this one of the great Characters of the spirit of *Antichrist*, that he exalts himself above all that is called God? and wherein hath he done this more remarkably towards Magistrates who are called Gods amongst men, then by exalting himself over them to become a Judge of all their Rights and pretentions to power in this world? We must therefore beware of entertaining the motions and practises of his Spirit, whereof this is a very eminent one, to judge of the Right of power to Rule in the world.

Nor doth God allow in the Word, those whom he hath made Subjects to Superior Powers, to take upon them to judge of the Rights & titles of those that are over them. The Rule of Subjects behaviour as Subjects is clearly determined in *Rom.* 13.1, till 8. & 1 *Pet,* 2. 13, 14. & *Tit.* 3. 1. Where we find nothing but a command of submission & subjection, of not resisting, and of paying taxes & dues, and of giving honour, fear and respect for Conscience sake unto Superiour powers, because they are Gods Ordinance over privat men, and they bear not the sword which God hath put in their hand, in vain. Now the Commandements thus delivered, without any limitation or restriction of their Rights to rule, or of our obedience (further then that we are bound to obey God rather than man) I suppose do oblige all Subjects that are under them, either to obey, or to suffer patiently if they find cause to refuse obedience; but that privat men in outward and humane concernments; and for worldly considerations of their own taking up, should not find any cause to refuse obedience, I conceive is the meaning of those absolute and unlimited injunctions which the Scripture layes upon Subjects, in respect of their Superior powers; so then the duty which God hath appointed Subjects to observe towards those that are over them, in the places of power, is clearly inconsistent with the scrupulositie of this question, concerning their Right and Title to Rule. Nor should those that are in places of power suffer their titles by meer private Subjects to be questioned; for either they should actually suppresse the disputes & disquiries of that nature in privat men, as not at all belonging to their cognizance, or they should prevent it in others who are to be accounted their equals, & to whom in reason they are accountable of their proceedings (for God hath made no men so Supreme, as not to be accountable unto others in a reasonable way) by some satisfactory declarations or demonstrations of the grounds of their Right to their places & of the equity of their proceedings therein. Nor lastly, can it stand with sound Reason or a good conscience in any privat man, to take upon him to be a Judge of that matter, & to suspend his acts of obedience in things otherwise good & lawfull in themselves, till his scruples in that kinde be satisfied. For first, no sound reason will allow any man to take upon him the judicature of rights, whereof it is not obvious to him, to know the true grounds circumstantially; & seeing al claims to places amongst men depend upon the concurrences of many circumstances, which in the way of justice give to one & take away from another a right to the same; & it is in Gods hand alone, to order the incidency of those circumstances between those that have power, and the competitors for the same places: & privat men cannot possibly in their ordinary way (wherein they are bound to stand and walk) know assuredly the incidencies of these circumstances, which change the nature of rights and claimes to places; therefore no justice nor reason can allow privat men to be Iudges of things whereof it is not morally possible for them to have a true insight, and whereinto they have no calling by God or men to make a speciall inquiry, without which they become unreasonably and unconscionably presumptuous, if they settle within themselvs, or utter towards others any judgement definitively. Then in the second place, it is a most unconscionable practice in any whom God hath put in the place of subjection, and of living in a private station, to resist the powers that are over him, requiring good and lawfull things, onely because he is not satisfied in their right to require those things of him, and in their Title to their places, as if Superiour Powers that are actually in the posession o places, which God hath put in their hands to rule others by, and serve the publick with, were accountable to every private man, concerning their right, by which they stand under God in their Charges, and as if it were lawfull for men professing Christianity, to dispense with matters of duty in themselves commendable and profitable to common edification, onely because they will appear opposite for some worldly respects unto those that are over them, to whom they owe due respect and submission.

Now

Now after all this; if you say: what? shall private Christians then make themselves slaves, to any that will rule over them; without judging rationally, who are their lawfull Superiours to whom they owe obedience, I say to this, no: for Christians are the only free men of the world: all the rest are slaves to their proper passions, lusts, opposite interests; but he that is subject to the law of liberty, doing all by a Rule; is truly free and none but he. But you will say; by what rule then shall he discern, who is his superior? I answer by a rule agreeable to sense, to reason, and to conscience. Sense will shew him who is actually in possession of all power and places of Government over him, and by this he will perceive under whom he doth stand. Reason will shew what he who is over him pretends unto; whether yea or no, his pretences are backed with power to maintain his right against all adversaries therein? and whether yea or no, the use of that power be limited by law; or left wholly to his own will without any law? And Conscience will shew that he to whom God hath committed the plenary administration, of publick affairs with unconfrontable power, is Gods vicegerent over the society of those to whom his administration doth extend it self, either by vertue of a contract, which makes a law, or by vertue of a conquest, which is bound to no law but the will of the Conqueror; for if the Apostle doth teach us that [all soules ought to be subject to the higher powers] because [there is no power but of God] and because [the powers that be] in place [are ordained of God] then it will follow, that those who are actually supreme, and in a plenary possession of power, ought to be obeyed as Gods Ordinance; for it is not possible that any can attain to the height of power without Gods disposall of it into his hands. Here then a Christian rests, and freely performs his duty toward him in all things good and lawfull, and makes no further inquiry, after the rights & titles according to lawes of men; because he doth consider that the most high giveth the Kingdomes of men to whomsoever he pleaseth. Thus keeping my Spirit from flying out beyond his bounds one way, and following the directions of a clear rule another way; I prevent this example wherewith you trouble your self without cause, and intangle your Conscience against your duty.

But here again it may be said, if this bee the condition of subjects, and if their duty toward Superiors is thus circumscribed; what way is there left for them to be freed from the unnaturall usurpation of tyrannicall powers? I answer there be three ways which God hath left to the reason of men to make use of, partly to prevent, partly to redresse the tyrannicall usurpations of an over ruling Roman. The first is, to settle subordinate Officers under him without whom he cannot act. The second is, to settle lawes whereby to circumscribe him, and their actings; and a law making power to whom both he and they are to be accountable. And the third is, the great and invincible law of necessity, whereof every one is so far the judge in his own cause and in his own place, as he is moved

moved thereby to venture his life and welfare to obſerve the dictates thereof; by theſe means ſubjects without judging of the titles of Superiours, may repreſſe the undue uſurpation of power in tyrannicall ſpirits: where you may take notice that although you and I, as private men ought not to make our ſelves judges of the rights which ſuperiors pretend to have in & to their places; yet that they are not without a judicature over them in thoſe places: for the ſubordinate Officers belonging to a ſtate are bound to judge of the rights of thoſe that are over them; both by which they ſtand in their places of ſupremacy, and by which they proceed in their actings toward ſubjects, leaſt they be made the inſtruments of Arbitrary power and Tyranny, and then alſo the law-making power, which in all Nations reſides by the law of Nature, in the convention of the Repreſentatives of the whole body of the people (whether it be made up of the heads of families, or of choſen Deputies who are intruſted with a delegated power from all the reſt) doth make or unmake rights in all places and perſons within it ſelf, as it from time to time doth ſee cauſe. As for the Law of neceſſity which begetteth war, whereby God is immediately appealed unto by thoſe that pretend to have no Superiors on earth, that he may judge of their rights; whatſoever his hand doth determine in the event, is to be counted the right of thoſe in favour of whom the determination is made by his judgement.

By theſe rules then quiet your mind according to your place, concerning the right, which the preſent powers have to Rule, do not take upon you to define matters whereof you are no competent judge; you are made a competent judge only of your own actions which belong to a ſubject, as you are under a viſible and uncontroulable power which God hath ſet over you, and your duty is to ſubmit thereunto, in all things agreeable to the will of God, judging your ſelf that you put no ſtumbling block, or an occaſion of offence in any mans way, Rom. 14:13: yet I will not ſay but in the judgement of diſcretion as you are a member of this Common-wealth, and concerned in the publick welfare thereof, you may look upon your ſuperiours to ſee how they pretend to ſtand: that is, by what apparent right, and with what viſible power they poſſeſs their places, but this you ought not to do ſo peremptorily, as to oblige your conſcience as to be ſuſpended upon the obſervations which you ſhall happen to make of them, and their proceedings; as if your private judgement in ſuch caſes ſhould be the Rule by which you ought to walk in point of obedience: I ſay you ought not to ſet up this judgement of yours ſo high within your ſelf and over others as to drown the thoughts of all other rules: but you ought to limit it as I have ſaid before, within the bounds of Chriſtianity, and diſcreet rationallity: wherein that I may help you yet a little further: Conſider ſoberly with your ſelf what can be anſwered to this plea, which they will alleadge for themſelves.

2. Whether

the present Engagement.

1. Whether yea or no, the Nationall tye and association, by which we were a Common-wealth while we were yet called a Kingdome, hath ever been dissolved.

2. If it hath not been dissolved, what hath kept it entire in the middest of all these shakings? was it not a Parliament? and the subordination of all Officers throughout the nation under it?

3. And if a Parliament is still remaining, and all subordinate Officers in places of judicature and execution, stand under it throughout the whole nation, so that all men may have a legal protection from injuries; what is there wanting to a lawfull power and government?

4. If nothing be wanting to a legall protection, for those that acknowledge the jurisdiction, then such as acknowledge it not, do put themselves out of that protection: and if they resist the power which God hath set over them for the publick good, and which is actually & fully possest with al the places of publick administration, they resist the Ordinance of God; and they that resist this Ordinance (saith the Apostle) shall receive to themselves damnation, *Rom.* 13. 2.

As for the point of enquiry, how these particular men in whose hands the power and government is, are come to their present places, whether in a legall way, or that which you call usurpation, it doth not belong to the Conscience of any man, who is in a private station, to determine peremptorily, far lesse upon his determination to suspend his actings towards the publique good. Yet if in this also you desire to reflect upon the passages of Right, without oblieging your Conscience to stand engaged either way by that which you shall observe, I shall further suggest these heads of matters applicable unto the case of those whom you suspect to be usurpers, unto your impartiall meditation, as a Plea which they do alledge for themselves.

First, Whether yea or no, it be any way unjust by the law of Nature, among men that are equals, to resist force with force?

Secondly, If it be just among equals to resist force with force, the second point will be to consider, Whether he that invades another mans naturall right, or he that defends his own, is to be accounted the Usurper?

Thirdly, If he that invades and seeks to deprive another man of his right, be the Usurper; then he that by resistance is deprived of that whereof he attempted to deprive his neighbour, is not wronged by way of usurpation, but justly defeated of the power which he did abuse.

Now they will say, that the case was thus first between the King and Parliament, if you count them Equals (which is the least can be given, say they, to a Parliament by the Law of Nature and Nations) and then afterward between the one party and the other in the Parliament, the same case was acted again, as between Equals: whereupon the City Militia on the one hand, and the Army on the other was depending, and set on work for action. And how far (these powers having dashed) those that prevailed did think themselves necessitated to settle the safety of the Common-wealth in their own way, and what settlement that hath by Gods permission brought forth, and upon what ground it now stands, I shall not need to represent unto you: only the sober consideration of the grounds which the party accused of usurpation, doth alleadge for its proceedings, are to be thought upon indifferently, without *prajudicat affectus*, if you will free your Conscience from a snare.

And this shall suffice also, concerning the first branch of your second doubt: but let us now come to the second branch thereof, which supposing the power to be usurped, doth question how far by taking the Engagement, you become accessary to the guilt thereof?

To this question, I shall answer briefly thus. That the Engagement being a duty, just to be required by the present Powers from their subjects; without the performance of which, there is no protection due unto them; and necessary to be performed by all, that will not professe themselves desirous to overthrow the present safety and publique wellfare of the nation: it cannot make those that take it accessary to the guilt of those that tender it, if any be in them; because the performance of a thing good in it self, and just and necessary for me to do in reference unto others, can derive no guilt before God from others, of the evill which may be in them, upon me. All Morall actions are to be counted good or evill, lawfull or unlawfull, according to the justice of the rule by which they are done, and according unto the usefulnesse and conveniency of the imediate and proper end, for which they are done: and if both these be found in the Agent thereof, no guilt can from without be brought upon him, by any co-Agents.

Now the Rule of Justice in this case, is, That we are bound to shew fidelity unto these of whom we desire protection: And that we are bound to be ready to every good work, towards those with whom we live, which is all that in the present state of this common-wealth is required of us; which if we desire not to performe, we deserve not to have a being in it: and if we desire to performe this, there can be no cause why we should not professe it, or why the profession of our willingnesse to do this should make us guilty of other mens sins.

As concerning the end for which the Engagement is to be taken, it is to oblege all to entend one and the same publique good, so far as in the present constitution of affairs, it may be advanced: and to give the Supreme Power an assurance that we shall not betray it, but that we are willing to maintain all good intelligence for publiqe Governments with it, notwithstanding the present changes brought upon the Common-wealth.

Suppose those that have the present Power had without any apprehension of necessity for common safety or danger to their own safety and liberty, only for

some

some sinister ends usurped the places wherein they are, yet by Gods permissions and direction over me, they being now therein, and finding themselves oblieged by their places to procure peace and unity among the subjects of this Land, and to preserve the publique interest for the good of all, according to their best understanding, if they use any expedient which doth tend thereunto, and offer it unto me to concur with them therein, with what Conscience can I refuse a concurrence to such an intention? If they having done amisse formerly, set themselves now to do well, can I with any conscience oppose them therein? Is it just or pious, that because they found no safety in the way by which I would have setled the Common-wealth, and have altered it, that therefore I should refuse to concur with them henceforth in any other way or at their motion do any thing, although it may be found never so usefull and necessary in it self for the good of the Common-wealth? If they were guilty one way (as you imagine) by taking upon them more then they had right to do: take heed least you be more guilty another way, by refusing to do that which before God and men you are oblieged to do: if you are afraid of pertaking of their sin, then take heed that you disturb not the publique welfare as much or more by this sin, then they did by that: If their guilt was by the usurpation of power to dissolve the way of settlement wherein we were, take heed lest you obstruct al other ways which henceforth may be taken towards a happy settlement only by the refusall of due subjection unto the power that is now over you, because you think your self or your party wrongfully deprived of the power which you had. If you strive for power as much as you think they have done, then you are more accessary to their usurpation by doing that your self for which you condemn them, then by yeelding to any lawfull Engagement for the good of the Common-wealth, which they propose unto you. Thus while you pretend to avoid a doubtfull guilt of another mans sin, least it reflect upon you; you contract an undoubted guilt of your own sin, by refusing a necessary duty to the Common-wealth. The truth is, they cannot be said guilty of Usurpation of Power; for it was by all the Authority of the Common-wealth that then was, both of King and Parliament, put into their hands, but if their guilt lies any where, it is this, that they abused their power: now you cannot be made accessary to this abuse thereof, which is already part, if you give not your expresse consent and approbation to that which they did, which I am confident they will never urge any man to do, who will promise henceforward to be faithfull to the peace and prosperity of this state, for some of the councell of State themselves, would not be ingaged to approve of all proceedings past, and yet sit still in councell with them to advance the publick welfare in time to come, wherby you may perceive that by this engagement they mean not to draw in others to be accessary, to their past proceedings, but to know who they are that are faithful in the land, & willing to concur

C 3

in good and lawfull undertakings in due time: for this is all that the engagement can rationally be stretcht unto, and he that wil not admit of it in this sense makes himself actually lyable to a greater sin then that which he pretends to be afraid to fall into], which is a way of proceeding very preposterous and unconscionable of sin for fear of being found sinfull.

Hitherto I have insisted upon your two first doubts, more largely then I did purpose at first, therefore in the third and last, I shall be more brief, for if in the two former you be well satisfied concerning that which is your duty, I cannot see how in this last you can be much further scrupled, for if your conscience is[once throughly convicted] of the lawfulnesse and necessitsy of a duty, it must cast [the events & consequences upon the performance of Gods providence, and not by the conjecturall appearances of your own apprehensions, in the ballance therewith. In the third doubt you say the [consequence of the engagement seems to tend to the opposition of two things] first to[exclude the lawfull heir of the crown from his right]; Secondly [to exclude the Lords from sitting in Parliament]to which things you say, you [are preingaged, and from which you cannot recede.] To which I shall offer these considerations to your more deliberate judgement. First, if those be only seeming inconveniences, and the other a certain and undoubted conveniency, nay a necessary and a dispensable duty, your conscience cannot justly suspend the latter for the formers sake, for there is no proportion of obligation in respect of conscience, between that which is seeming a, and that which is undoubtedly certain, we are commanded [not to judge according to appearances but to judge righteous judgement] Joh: 7.24:by which we must conclude that to follow appearances; is not to follow the rules of righteousnesse, and consequently, that it is not conscionable to act unrighteous, or to suspend righteous actings, only for appearances of evill, and as it is absurd to do evill that good may come of it : so it is also unconscionable to leave off the doing of that which is infallibly good, that no doubtfull evill may come of it; & then consider the duty which you refuse to do; relates to the whole Common-wealth, the safety of all, and your own necessary peace and preservation, and the evill which you fear will come upon it, relates only to the seeming violation, of a perticular right of some few persons which is, or may be doubtful, whether you be any further engaged thereto yea or no, for when you say that you are preingaged so that you cannot recede; I must suppose that you mean not a wilfull but a conscionable preingagement, and that you cannot lawfully recede from it: but if the contrary hath already appeared and is cleer to your conscience now, that your duty and preingagement to the whole Common-wealth cannot lawfully and conscionably be put in the ballance, with a perticular engagement to some persons depending thereon ; then you cannot make any further doubt of that which should be done in this case : for I cannot imagine that

you

you will think it lawfull for you to dispute your interest toward the universall good of the Common-wealth, for any perticular engagement though never so strong otherwise, and lawfully undertaken at first: for if the interest of him, who you call the heir of the crown, and of the men called the Peers of the Kingdom, is of so much weight with you, that you will do no good also to the Common-wealth without them: then it is clear, that in your esteem they are more then the Commonwealth to you, and that the common cause, for the maintaining of which a'l your engagements, are wrought upon you is not so much valued by you, as the perticular cause of these persons, which how you can with a good conscience allow in your self, I am not able to understand. I say then that if the particular interests and pretentions of any, come to justle with the publick good in your affections, and justle out the same, it is clear that you are not faithfull to your principles of conscience and reason before God and men, but that you are willing to betray the common cause to particular designs and consequently that you will seek your self in the bottome more then the publick good: because it cannot be doubted, that if you will subordinate your zeal and love to the common-wealth unto the respect which you have to other mens advantages, that you will far more if occasion be offerd, subordinate the same unto the respect which you have to your own advantages. For the rsolution of this scruple (you ought as I conceive to understand your self thus far, that you cannot entertaine the thought of any engagement or obligation lawfully, which doth cause your engagement and obligation, to be true and faithfull to the Commonwealth, at all times or at any time, therefore with a good conscience, if you find your obligation to the heir of the crown, or to the Priviledges of Peers, fall crosse and oppposit by change of circumstances (as all human matters are changeable by circumstances) to the common good of the nation; (I say) you cannot in such a case maintain that obligation so, as not to be receded from it with a good conscience: and if the proposall of this engagement, doth discover thus much of your corruption unto you by such a scruple, you are to be humbled for it before God; and laying aside henceforth all Hypocrisie, rectifie the intentions of the heart with uprightnesse and sincerity. And all this I offer to be considered by you, supposing your preingagement to have been just and lawfull, as no doubt it was, but yet that now your resolution not to recede from it, cannot be stil just and lawfull as matters now stand in the state, if you will make that preingagement to justle out of your affection this engagement, which now is offered unto you to be taken.

    As for the dissolution of your tie and obligation to the heir of the crown, I shall refer you to look upon God, whether he hath not dispossessed him wholly by his own doings and councells, and by the guilt derived from his father and mother upon, himself all his interest in this Kingdom, and Common-wealth: for

because

Considerations concerning

because his aim and the aim of those that are about him is not for the Common wealth, but for the Kingdom, that is not for the good of the society: but for selfegreatness.

Therefore God, who takes and gives the Rights of Government by the putting of one into the actuall possession of a ruling power, and by taking of the same power away from another, to fulfill his own counsell and judgements over this people, and over those that exalt themselves over them by destroying the earth, he hath done as it seemeth good in his own eyes, both with him who according to men claims the Crown, and with those that were the supporters thereof, more then promoters of the publique good: And what God who doth exalt one and put downe another, determines in this kind, in the sight of all the world, and (I may say) against the clear intentions of all that engaged themselves at first for the good of the Nations, and for the Kings good also; what I say, he determines thus in this kind against mens intentions and expectations, whose affections have been sincerely set for the Kings just Rights, no lesse then yours you and I have no warrant to contradict or oppose in our thoughts: but we must observe this way of changing the rights, and shaking the titles of the earth, that the Lord alone may be exalted in the day of our common, and their speciall visitation; for I conceive that the Prophecy of the Prophet *Isaiah, cap.24.v.21.* is begun to be fulfilled amongst us, somewhat more remarkably then in other parts of the earth as yet, which is this: *And it shall come to passe in that day, that the Lord shall punish the host of the high ones that are on high, and the Kings of the Earth upon the ea th; and they shall be gathered together as prisoners are gathered in the pit, and shall be shall be shut up in prison, and after many dayes shall be visited. Then then the Moon shall be confounded and the Sun ashamed, when the Lord of hosts shall reign in mount Sion and before his ancients gloriously.* I shall not now stand to open these words unto you further then their sense is obvious, to shew that which with another ear the same Prophet saith, to the same or like effect, *That the lofty looks of men shall be humbled, and the haughtinesse of men bowed down, and the Lord alone shall be exalted in that day; for the day of the Lord of hosts shal be on every one that is proud & lofty, and upon every one that is lifted up, and he shall be brought low:* which is a warning also to those that are now exalted in power over us; lest they be high minded in their own conceits & their ruin come suddenly, & without remedy, if they all or any of them wil as Israel once did say to the seers, see not, & to the Prophets prophecy not right things unto us; prophecy deceits, & cause the holy one of Israell, & his law to cease from before us, & if when they begin to despise his word (as some of them otherwise very active & instrumental in outward changes seem to do) they trust then in oppression, and perversenesse, & lean upon their word and stay thereod, they must take notice, they shall be taught to

know

know with dear experience, if they alter not their course; *Esa.* 50. 11. 12.13. that this iniquity shall be to them as a breach ready to fall, swelling out in a high wall, whose breaking commeth suddenly and at an instant; for if the tallest Cedars are not spared, but cut down, when they exalt themselves above the Trees of the Forrest: how shall the smaller shrubs be borne withall, when they are guilty of the same misdemeanor? they therefore that stand before the Lord of the whole earth, let them be wise and feare; he standeth among the Gods and judgeth : even he, who being the King of Kings, came to serve all men through love, and doth teach all men to deny themselves, and deceive his Disciples; learne of him that he is meeke, and humble of heart. If they seeke themselves and not the Common-wealth, whereunto they pretend to engage others; they shall be found out by those whom they engage to the Interest of the Common-wealth, who mind it sincerely; and being discovered, they shall be cast out of their greatness in it. We have seene severall parties up, and their severall Interests set a foot; and their changes came, because the true Interest of Christianity, wherein all Common-wealths alone can prosper, hath not been so much minded by them as their own Interests, we should therefore pray for those that are over us now, that though they may have had, and have stil their failings, yet that they may not be split upon this Rock, and we should watch also over our own soules, least we be made a cause of their own splitting, and of the ruine of all, by being intised to be wilfully scrupulous in these matters; as perhaps some are for ends of their own, to make the way of Government difficult, and the standing of those that are in places of power unsafe : If any be such (of which number I know you are none) they shall eat of the fruits of their own doings assuredly. For if they acknowledg the jurisdiction deceitfully to betray it; God will find them out, if they will not acknowledg it, nor any thing (though never so good) offered to the publick interest by it; onely because they will keep mens spirits at a distance from it: they shall not escape to be consumed by the fire, which they do maliciously kindle to destroy the Common-wealth : if the common interest, which I am perswaded, is in simplicity to be aimed at by the engagement, according to their sense that offer it; were without scrupulosity and contradiction taken up and intended by all; what an easie matter would it be in a short time to bring at last about a reall Reformation of all our grievances; but if those that complain of pressures and grievances, and of the charge of an Army, by their own disaffection to the publick, and unrulines under Government, make an Army absolutely necessary, and occasion the grievances themselves, whereof they

D   make

make complaints onely to caſt an odium upon the Government: they will be found to be the Children of their Father the Devill, and receive with him their reward; for he obſtructs all that is good in every one, and tempts all unto diſtempers and diſorderly Carriages, and then layes them to their Charge to make them odious thereby. Beſides the ſcruples which you have made in this buſineſs, I have met with ſome, that labour to make ſtrange interpretations and inferences upon every word of the Engagement, as if it were in the meaning of thoſe that offer it, a bundle of ſnares; but trouble not your ſelf with that, for in all promiſes of this kind, the Rule is, that you muſt take the ſenſe which is moſt obvious, to expreſs an undeniable duty; and by following this, you ſhall not be intangled into ſcruples and ſuſpitions, what others may ſtrain the words unto. Another told me, (and if I underſtand by him that many are thus ſcrupled) that although he could take the Engagement in a lawfull ſenſe, and approve the obvious ſenſe of it; yet that he ought not to do it, by reaſon of the offences, which many godly people would take at him for it, who cannot but think it a breach of Covenant. To this I anſwered, that in a neceſſary matter of duty, an offence wrongfully taken at it, ought not to be regarded by thoſe that perform it; but they ought rather to follow their own Conſcience, and give to thoſe that are offended at them in their way, a ſatisfactory reaſon of the juſtice thereof, to inſtruct them; but in things of an indifferent nature, which are free to be done or left undone, there we are bound to ſuſpend the action which may be taken offenſively: as for this matter I ſay, that on both hands there will be offences given, or taken, and that by the Godly. For as ſome godly will be offended at the taking of the Engagement, ſo ſome others will be offended, at the not taking thereof: the caſe then will be which of theſe two offences I am moſt to avoid; whether that which is wrongfully, or that which is juſtly taken, both by the godly, and alſo by thoſe that are in ſuperiority; whom I offend, ſo as to give them juſt cauſe, to deny unto me for my offence their protection, and my neceſſary ſafety, and us here, of the ſame act: the offence on the one hand is ſinfully given, and on the other wrongfully taken; it is eaſie to judge which of the two is to be avoided. I ſhall leave theſe things to your conſcionable and unprejudicat conſideration, to be weighed in the feare of God by you; as in his preſence without humane reſpects they are offered to you, by

From my Chamber *Your faithfull and affectionate Friend*
Novemb. 27. 1649. *in Chriſt.* I. D.

F I N I S.

The grosser faults.

Page 1. line 4. read to serve you. P.8. l.9. r. uttered, p.9.l.20.r. Right to suspend the use of it at this time. I may, nay I ought to resolve to abstaine from the prosecution of a Right, p.15.l.29.r. for example, r. scruple, l.36. for Roman, read Power, p.18. l.2. read clashed, l. 7. read affections, l.37.for Governments, read concernments, p.19.l.33. read past, p.20.l.5. read to sin, l.11. read of the performance upon, l. 12. read lay, l.19. read undispensible, p.21. l.1. read dispense with you, l.8. read brought, l. 21. read Crosse, l.25. read matters, l.34. of your heart, p.22. l.29. read in another place, l.41. read Sword and stay thereon, p. 23. l. 10. read become his Disciples learning, p. 24. l.13. read, and I understand, l.29. read, and where, of the

The extract of the LETTER, containing the further SCRUPLE against the ENGAGEMENT.

I Took advantage by this Bearer to intreat the favour of Mr. *Dury*, in a few lines to desire his judgement in the subscription now pressed. I hear it is come into our County, and I perceive it a great trouble to many godly well-meaning men; who do fear their former Solemne Obligations do so lye upon them, that they cannot go back from what their lips have uttered; unlesse those said Engagements were manifestly sinfull, which yet appears not; as also, they fear this Government was not chosen (truly) by the People, nor (truly) by their Representatives. This I dare say is indeed a Scruple, and not peevishnesse or faction, nor sedition in these I meane; but they feare sinning against God: and they look at this as a rack of Conscience truly so called; yet it were better to suffer then sin; of which till satisfaction be given, we resolve to take heed. I pray pardon this boldnesse, &c.

The Answer to the fore-named Extract.

SIR,

IN the Letter which you have written to *N. N.* you desire my judgment concerning the subscription to the present Engagement, now pressed; To give you satisfaction, I shall relate what I did, when I conceived that I was bound, either to declare my assent thereunto: or a reason wherefore I could not do it. First, I reflected upon this assertion as a Rule; *That if the obvious sense of a promise, required of me, by any to whom I am obliged to give an Answer, doth containe a clear and undeniable duty; that then I am obliged to make that promise, if those that offer it, do not contradict the sense wherein I think I am bound to make it,* Having laid this ground for my proceeding, in the second place, I did consider the words of the Engagement in the sense which I thought most obvious, and most agreeable to the duty of a peaceable Christian, & good Common-weakhs-
man,

man: and that sense I set down in writing, as you see in the adjoyned paper.

This writing I did shew to some of those who are in Chief Authority, Authors of the framing of the Engagement, and intrusted by the Parliament to propose it unto all: they declared that this meaning was satisfactory; and thereupon I found my selfe obliged in conscience to engage thereunto. If the ground which I did lay is sound, and the manner of proceeding sure and inoffensive; if the words of the Engagement beare this obvious sense; and if this sense is a clear Duty, no wayes contradictory to any former Engagements wherein you have opened your mouth to the Lord, then I do not see what should give you cause to scruple, except it be that those who propose it unto you, declare that this meaning is not satisfactory, and that something else is intended by the Engagement, which I am confident none ought to do. As for the scruples which are raised about the seeming contradiction between this and former Engagements, I suppose they will be taken off by this adjoyned printed paper, which you may be pleased to peruse, and to offer to your Brethren, that are not pewish as you call it, but stand off for fear of sinning, and if after the impartiall Consideration thereof, any scruple doth remain further with your selfe or any, I should be glad to know of it; where the stop in their spirit doth lye; and you will do me a pleasure to acquaint me therewith; for I think it my duty to help to remove it. As for that point of scruple, which you intimate in your letter to be the maine thing, that they fear this Government was not chosen truly by the People, nor truly by their Representatives: although this cannot be denyed, that neither the People, nor their Representatives, as such did chuse this way of Government, yet seeing by Gods providence how it is the Government in being, & seeing I am taught by the Apostle to believe, (*Rom.* 13 1.) That there is no governing power but of God, and that the Powers which be in Government are ordained of God to be over me; & that therefore I ought to be in subjection under them, by doing things holy, and just, and peaceable, tending to the Publick Good in my calling; therefore I conceive my selfe no wayes obliged to stumble at the way of their coming to their places of Government, after they are once in a plenary possession thereof, as being no competent

(25)

~~shall Judge~~ of the ~~rises~~ of ~~power~~, and ~~rights to places~~ of ~~superiority~~. This I must leave to them, and to God, in due ~~time to~~ judge; but yet this may be said for the present ~~Governours~~; that those who remained in the House, were, and are ~~still in the places~~, whereunto they were lawfully ~~chosen~~, and wherein from the beginning they stood as true Representatives: nor can any thing to my understanding be alleadged, why they that remained, and were not cast out of their places ~~by the force which the~~ Army used, should ~~loose their right~~ to govern, or leave off to administer the Common-wealth the best way they can: and what although it may be suspected that some of them had a hand in stirring up the Army to cast out their Brethren; yet when matters are fallen from a peaceable way of government which the people had chosen to a warlike Constitution of affaires; and in cases of breaches between those that are equally in the possession of Supream Power, when their parties are formed, and have attempted to act against one another by force for the driving on of opposite designes: yet (I say) in such cases and at such times, the violent proceedings of some against their Brethren who had violent attempts also against them, (though I excuse neither but both may be faulty in something) doth not dissolve the originall right to govern which was in either of them by their first choise, wherein they were made Representatives: it is indeed the misery of a Nation when their Representatives in government fall thus at odds within themselves, and bring a necessary and fatall change upon the Government: but yet we must observe that in times of such division & distraction, every change of Government, doth not dissolve the right which is in those to who the care of publick administration is remitted to do for the publick good, that which they shall think necessary & expedient to be done, according to the circumstances of times & places. The irregularity of some in the use of power doth not deprive others of their right to discharge their duty in the places wherein they are set. Although then the Government is not that which the people hath by any universall and unanimous consent chosen (for that is not possible to be had as matters now stand) yet it is that which their Representatives in place, and possession of their right to govern have chosen: and this should quiet my private way of judgement, if I will not presume above my line.

I shall

I shall beseech the Lord, to make us in these times of tryall, to know the perfect way wherein we ought to walk, without blame before him in love; and the Lord blesse you in your Ministery, and make all that are upright, in heart free from prejudices against their Brethren; that salvation may come out of *Sion*. Remember me in your thoughts, and prayers for the peace thereof, who am in Christ,

St. *James* this 18. December. 1649

Your Brother and servant in the Gospel, John Dury.

The Wordes of the Engagement.	The Meaning thereof which is a Duty.
I do declare and promise, that I shall be true and faithfull	I do in expresse words oblige my self, and am hereby really engaged, That sincerely and uprightly, without any mentall reservation, and honestly without any deceitfull purpose; I shall with all affectionate care & diligence, to the utmost of my abilities seek and procure.
To the Common-Wealth of England,	The Common-good, the Peace and publick welfare of the People of this Land in their Nationall Association.
As the same is now established,	Which at this time doth stand under the power & Government of the Parliament & Counsell of State that now is.
Without a King and House of Lords.	Although there is no single Person ruling in chief; nor company of Peers sitting as a Body in this Government.

FINIS